The world su... sensation I would remember when I wrote *Hatchet*. With the dying of the engine every aspect of our flight drastically altered. No longer was the forest sliding by beneath us wonderful scenery; it had become a place that would try to wreck the plane, try to freeze us, try to starve us, try to end us. I had spent a lot of time in the bush but it was always at my own behest, when I wanted to be there and in the condition I wanted to be in. Now I was falling, and falling fast, toward a wilderness I was unprepared to deal with; I had the wrong clothes, no weapon, no survival gear except for a sleeping bag and the plane's emergency kit. In a very real way, I had become the Brian Robeson I would soon write about.

ALSO BY GARY PAULSEN

GUTS

THE TRUE STORIES BEHIND *HATCHET* AND THE BRIAN BOOKS

GARY PAULSEN

Published by
Dell Laurel-Leaf
an imprint of
Random House Children's Books
a division of Random House, Inc.
1540 Broadway
New York, New York 10036

Visit us on the Web! www.randomhouse.com/teens

Educators and librarians, for a variety of teaching tools, visit us at www.randomhouse.com/teachers

ISBN: 0-440-40712-5

RL: 6.4

Reprinted by arrangement with Delacorte Press

Printed in the United States of America

November 2002

10 9 8 7 6 5 4 3 2 1

OPM

This one's for Boogie.

CONTENTS

FOREWORD

I've written about a boy named Brian Robeson in four books: *Hatchet, The River,
Brian's Winter* and *Brian's Return*. Most of the
mail I've received about these books has con-
sisted of questions about those parts of my
personal life that paralleled Brian's. To ad-
dress such questions in general terms I wrote
Father Water, Mother Woods: Essays on Fishing

and Hunting in the North Woods, which tells of my childhood hunting and fishing and some of what I learned in the woods.

But the result was that the mail, far from settling down, actually increased. So many readers demanded to know specific incidents—when and where I was attacked by a moose, or how the plane crashed or was forced down, or how I killed a deer, as Brian did, or whether the mosquitoes really attacked me as they attacked Brian—that I felt I should tell the stories that inspired Brian's adventures in the woods, just as they happened to me.

So much of what I did as a boy came to be part of Brian—all of it, in some ways. I hope that *Guts* satisfies those readers who want to know more about Brian and my life.

CHAPTER 1

HEART ATTACKS, PLANE CRASHES AND FLYING

He was sitting in the bushplane roaring seven thousand feet above the northern wilderness with a pilot who had suffered a massive heart attack and who was either dead or in something close to a coma.

He was alone. HATCHET

Perhaps the single most catastrophic event in Brian's life in *Hatchet* is when the pilot dies of a heart attack. This forces Brian to fly the plane and land—in little more than an "aimed" crash—in a lake, where he swims free and saves himself.

Before I was fortunate enough to become successful as a writer, I worked at home, writing as much as I could between construction jobs. Because I had so much downtime, I added my name to a list of volunteers available to answer emergency ambulance calls. My wife and I lived then in a small prairie town in the middle of farm country, near the confluence of two major highways. The volunteer service was small, and all we had was one old ambulance donated by a city that had bought new ones. But we were the only service available for thousands of square miles.

We answered calls to highway wrecks, farm accidents, poisonings, gunshot accidents and many, many heart attacks. I would go out on the calls alone or with another man who also worked at home.

I saw at least a dozen heart attack victims in the first year. Sadly, most of them were dead before I arrived. The distances we had to cover were so great that we simply could not get there in time to save them. If we did arrive before they died, we had to wait an hour or more for the "flight for life" chopper from the nearest city. Often it arrived too late.

When I came to write *Hatchet*, I remembered one call to a small ranch some sixty miles northeast of Colorado Springs. It was early in the morning when the siren cut loose, and I ran half-dressed for my old truck, drove to the garage where the ambulance was kept and answered the phone hanging on the wall.

"Please come quick!" a woman said. "It's my Harvey. He's having chest pains."

She gave me the location of the ranch and I took off. It should have taken me a full twenty minutes to get there because of the roughness of the gravel roads but I arrived in fourteen by driving like a maniac.

It was just getting light as I ran into the house carrying our emergency bag, and I could smell what was happening as soon as I entered the kitchen. The lights were on and a man of about fifty was sitting at the kitchen table. His face was gray and he was holding his left shoulder with his right hand. He looked at me and smiled sheepishly, as if to apologize for the inconvenience, and started to say something but then stopped and looked again at the floor in what soldiers call the thousand-yard stare. His wife, a thin woman in jeans and a sweatshirt, stood by him, and she gave me what we called the Look—an expression that meant *Thank God you're here please save him please save him please save him.*

But the smell of methane was very strong and the gray look was very bad and as I reached for him to put him on his back, he jolted as if hit by electricity, stiffened in the kitchen chair and fell sideways to the floor. His eyes looked into mine. Directly into my eyes.

"Call the hospital and tell them to bring the chopper *now*," I said, and knelt to help him, but he was hit with another jolt that stiffened him and his eyes opened wide and the smell grew much stronger and I knew he was gone. There was, of course, hope—there is always hope. Even when I was called to car accidents and saw children I knew were dead, I would keep working on them because I could not bring myself to accept their death—the hope would not allow it—and I worked on this man now though the smell came up and the skin grew cold. I kept at the CPR because the woman kept giving me the Look and I could not give up hope. But minutes passed and then half an hour before I heard the sound of the rotors—which was very good time, though much too late for this man— and I kept working on him though I knew he was dead and I had seen him die, seen him move from his life into his death, and though

I had seen death many times before, I had not seen it in this way. Not in the way his eyes had looked into mine while the life left him.

Years later, when I came to write *Hatchet* and the scene where the pilot is dying, I remembered this man of all the men I saw dead from heart attacks and car wrecks and farm accidents. I remembered him and his eyes and I put him in the plane next to Brian because he was, above all things, real, and I wanted the book to be real. But I did not sleep well that night when I wrote him into the book and I will not sleep well tonight thinking of his eyes.

In some strange warp of fate I was to witness an airplane crash, or its immediate aftermath, almost exactly one week after that man died. This would also go into *Hatchet*.

Few people realize that the land rises southeast of Denver, just as it does to the west, where the Rockies lie. Grass hills slope gently upward, slightly higher than the Denver airport, for fifty or sixty miles, then taper off into the prairies of Kansas.

One pilot did not check his charts and took off from Denver at a low altitude, thinking that the ground would fall away gently below him. He hit the top six feet of a dirt ridge at 180 knots cruising speed. I was on the scene within four hours of the crash and the only recognizable item was the engine, a crumpled ball of steel and oil stains.

Everything else—the three passengers, who couldn't have known what hit them, the seats, the wings, the fuselage, everything—was torn and flattened and shattered. The bodies simply did not exist, not even as bits of pieces, and the investigative team finally gave up trying to make any sense from the crash. The debris, mechanical and human, extended from the ridge where the plane had first struck, spreading out in an oval a hundred yards wide and a quarter mile long. Most of the wreckage was in quarter- or half-dollar-sized pieces. Had the pilot flown a mere *six feet* higher, he would have been safe. Instead, the image of the destruction that resulted from a full-speed collision with the ground came back to me when I later wrote the scene in *Hatchet*.

I had seen other plane wrecks. I saw fighters crash when I was in the military—spectacular crashes, sometimes with the pilot dying, though more often ejecting safely—but those were extreme events with extreme machines and the dynamics would not necessarily apply here. Jet fighters at work, training or fighting, are always, always pushing their performance envelope, as are the pilots—they must be that way to stay alive in combat.

In 1946, when I was seven years old and on

a ship headed to the Philippines, I saw a passenger plane ditch in the Pacific. It was a C-54, a four-engine propeller-driven plane used for carrying freight and passengers during the Second World War. It was usually very reliable, but in this case there was some problem that affected all four engines and they had to ditch. The captain of our ship stopped in midocean, and the C-54 circled until the pilot could bring the plane in as close as possible to the ship. The ocean was nearly flat, or seemed so, but the plane appeared to skip when it first hit; then it moved slightly sideways in the air, then hit again and broke in two about two thirds of the way back to the tail. We were close enough to see people spilling out into the water, and when the plane settled down and stopped, more people emerged from the doors and onto the wing. They were all women and children—later we learned that they had been on their way to see their husbands and fathers—and at this point the loss of life was not so terrible. Even those thrown clear had life jackets on and were moving in the water, and the lifeboats from the ship were already lowered and on their way to pick up survivors.

But the ship was very slow—barely making seven knots—and full of people, and hence full of food garbage from the galley that was collected and then thrown off the stern each day. Sharks, dozens, scores, perhaps hundreds of them, were following the ship to eat the trash, and as soon as the plane hit the water the sharks made for the wreckage. The plane sank almost immediately, and in the minutes it took for the boats to reach the people, the sharks tore into them. It was as bad as anything I have ever seen. At times the sailors had to beat the sharks off and pull the people out of their mouths in a kind of horrible tug-of-war.

Later, when I was writing, I remembered the way the plane broke in two on the seemingly flat and still water; it was as if the plane had hit a brick surface instead of liquid. Research showed me that while large passenger planes almost always break in half on impact with water (depending on the height of the waves), single-engine or smaller planes almost never do. But I remembered the solidity of that impact when I came to write of Brian crashing the Cessna and the way the water might look soft but act like concrete.

Although I have never crashed in a Cessna 406 (and I hope I never do), I nearly crashed in one and have been in a forced landing in another, and both times it seemed I would certainly die.

Both incidents occurred in Alaska in the winter after I ran my second Iditarod Trail Sled Dog Race. After running the first I had written the novel *Dogsong*, which brought me some recognition. I was touring the state, talking in villages about writing and running dogs and flying from village to village in a Cessna 406 bushplane.

The pilot seemed very young, but then I was getting to an age when a lot of people seemed young, and he was very competent, and he did the preflight checks well, and though we were usually the only two on the plane, he always repeated his lecture about safety belts, the location of emergency gear and fire extinguishers and how to evacuate the plane. It was winter and we were heading to a village in the interior well north of Fairbanks. It was very cold—perhaps fifty below—and I had stupidly not brought parkas or proper winter clothing because in two days I was due to fly out of Anchorage back to the lower forty-eight. We were cruising at approximately three thousand feet over winter-clad forest. Now and then I could see a moose, once I thought I saw a wolf, and I was just musing about how much I truly loved the woods, the wildness of it, when the engine stopped.

It did not stop dead. Our forward progress kept the propeller turning, windmilling, but it was clear that the engine was no longer firing and we had gone dead-stick: no engines, no controls. The pilot immediately put the plane into a glide to keep up airspeed.

The world suddenly changed—and it was a sensation I would remember when I wrote *Hatchet*. With the dying of the engine every aspect of our flight drastically altered. No longer was the forest sliding by beneath us wonderful scenery; it had become a place that would try to wreck the plane, try to freeze us, try to starve us, try to end us. I had spent a lot of time in the bush but it was always at my own behest, when I wanted to be there and in the condition I wanted to be in.

Now I was falling, and falling fast, toward a wilderness I was unprepared to deal with; I had the wrong clothes, no weapon, no survival gear except for a sleeping bag and the plane's emergency kit. In a very real way, I had become the Brian Robeson I would soon write about.

The pilot was busy, trying to restart the engine, working to raise somebody on the radio, reviewing emergency procedures (pull the seat belt tight, protect your face), keeping the right glide angle to hold the plane in the air as long as possible and yet maintain flying speed, and all the while trying to locate a place suitable for an emergency landing.

In my own way, I was equally busy. While he worked with the plane I was thinking of what lay ahead, trying to deal with the unknown, trying not to think of the crashes I'd seen in the army, or of that long-ago plane hitting the water in the Pacific—although in northern Alaska's midwinter a water landing was the least of my concerns.

I needn't have worried. The plane was equipped both with wheels and with skis (the wheels protruded through holes in the skis) and the young pilot was very professional. The country below us was covered with small streams and rivers, all frozen into ribbons of white, and he picked one, pulled the flaps a bit, slipped the plane slightly down to the side and landed neatly and almost delicately on a river that at first seemed too narrow and then, as we approached the ground, appeared wide enough for a passenger jet. The plane slid easily on the snowpack over the river ice and settled and stopped.

"No worry," he said, taking a small tool kit from beneath the seat. "It'll just take a minute, happens all the time, just stay in your seat. . . ." And he jumped out, mumbling something about ice or oil or water in the gas. He had slipped a parka on and the hood muffled his voice.

Oh, I thought, oh, good. So we don't have to worry, because the engine-stopping happens all the time. That made me feel much better.

Off to the side of the frozen river I could see moose tracks going up the bank in the snow and they seemed fresh and I was thinking that if we were here very long, at least we would have meat—if there was a rifle in the emergency pack, or perhaps I could make a bow if we had much time; I had made bows before and hunted with them and the main thing was that we had matches and we were in woods so there was plenty of firewood and we could take a moose for meat and do well. . . .

But the pilot was as good as his word. In less than five minutes he climbed back into the cockpit, pumped the throttle and hit a switch or two and the engine roared to life.

"Water," I heard him yell over the engine noise. "Fuel line . . . condensation . . . bubble . . . clear . . ."

I nodded but knew little more than I had before except that the engine was running and sounded even and healthy. The part of the frozen river he had landed on was straight for another mile, with tree-covered hills fairly close on either side. He aimed the plane down the middle of the river and gunned the throttle. We seemed to leap off the snow and were airborne, flying on to the next village a hundred miles away. I watched the frozen forest slide by with new interest and when I wrote of Brian in the same seat, in the same plane, I remembered the feeling of the engine stopping and the propeller windmilling as the plane glided helplessly toward the earth.

The very next year I would gain intimate knowledge of another part of a 406 that Brian would come to know, the tail section, though in a drastically different way than Brian learned of it.

I was in my second Iditarod and it was brutal. I am not inordinately superstitious but this was the thirteenth running of the race and it seemed as if the whole thing was jinxed. The weather was absolutely appalling, with blizzards and wind so hard it would drive snow and ice particles into your eyes with the lids *closed*, at times sucking the air out of your lungs. I had run in bad weather, but never like this. At one point, in the middle of a blizzard in the dead middle of a dark night, I could not see one foot past the front of the sled, could not see a single dog or any part of a trail, and when the team stopped I crawled forward on my hands and knees (you couldn't stand without getting blown over) and found my lead dog, a great little three-year-old named Little Buck, trying to find the edge of the trail in the deep snow by feeling with his feet.

On top of this nightmare of weather there had been a foul-up and they had somehow failed to ship our dog food to the checkpoints. The first time it happened, the mushers got together and hired a helicopter to fly food in, though we had already paid for shipment. When it happened again, there was a three-day hold on the race while we all sat and waited for the food to arrive at drop points ahead of us. Eventually the race went on but the tempo (and yes, there *are* a flow and a plan to the race) was altered, perhaps destroyed. It became a clawing run to try to get in front and stay there.

Libby Riddles won the race, the first woman to do so, by heading across sea ice in wind and storm so strong that nobody else would attempt it. I tried a day after she left and my sled dogs blew back on top of me in a furry pile. Caught on the sea ice and unable to compete, I got word to Nome—by telling a musher, who told another musher, who told still another musher, who told a ham-radio operator at the checkpoint where I was—that I was ready to get off the ice. My handler, waiting in Nome, found a bushplane to come and get me and my dogs.

At first I could not believe that a plane could do that. I had heard stories about the amazing feats of bush pilots and their planes, but I always thought the tales were exaggerated, almost mythical.

The conditions have to be fully understood to appreciate what the pilot did. I'm not sure of the wind speed—I later heard that it was gusting to over ninety knots. All I know is that it was so powerful that it was impossible to stay on my feet. My dogs were tucked back in a pressure ridge with the sled jammed in at their rear. I lay with the dogs at my side and if I tried to go out and stand, the wind simply blew me flat or got beneath me and blew me away. Later I heard stories of men being blown off their sleds and out across the ice for several miles before they could stop. The only reason the dogs didn't blow away was that they were low and their claws could grip the ice. It had been rumored that an entire team had been blown away and was found by a plane two days later, forty-five miles away. This proved to be untrue but not one person doubted it at the time.

In this maelstrom of wind and blowing snow and ice the pilot left Nome, only ninety miles away, and came to find me. When he saw my bright yellow sled bag, he set the plane down on the ice near me and waved at me to come. He didn't land the plane so much as fly it down to the ice and hold it

there, the prop roaring and the nose into the
wind while he signaled me. Coincidentally,
the plane was another Cessna 406.

But I still could not stand up, and it
seemed an impossible thirty yards to the
plane. I crawled to my lead dog, the same Little Buck who had felt for the trail with his
toes, and pulled him out of his relative com-
fort in the ice ridge. Still on my hands and
knees, I dragged him and the rest of the team
over to the plane. But as soon as the sled
pulled clear of the scant protection of the
ridge (it was less than four feet high), the
wind took it and it spun out like a weather-
vane so that the dogs and I had all we could
do to drag it. I crawled back down the line of
fourteen dogs and used my knife to cut it
loose—it blew away, along with all my gear—
and then crawled back to the leader and
pulled him with me to the plane.

At the side I stood and opened the door,

holding on to a handle just inside, and pulled in the dogs, all still harnessed together. They had never been in a plane, or even close to one with the engine running, and for half a second it seemed that they would drag me off in their fear. But they have enormous trust, and Little Buck at last let me throw him up and through the door. With the leader inside, the rest of them decided to follow and allowed me to grab them by the backs of their harnesses and throw them into the plane. The problem was that while they trusted me, they were still terrified. The incredible roar of the engine was magnified by the wind so that the sound was truly deafening. To those dogs the inside of that plane was the most dangerous place in the world. They turned and ran away from the noise as fast as they could, into the tail of the plane.

Fourteen dogs, about fifty pounds each, meant that suddenly seven hundred pounds was jammed back in the tail, in a plane that was essentially already flying. The tail dropped like a stone and the plane seemed to hop about a hundred feet in the air. I had a tight grip on the handle by the door and had one leg inside when the plane jumped, and for what seemed an eternity I hung there, half out of the plane, before it snapped a little on a gust and tipped me up and in.

Thanks to the angle of climb caused by the weight in the tail, I tumbled back on top of the dogs, adding another two hundred pounds to the problem. I was upside down in a pile of dogs, all howling over the roar of the engine, when I heard the pilot scream, "There's too much weight in the tail! Throw the dogs forward or we're going down!"

I lunged to my feet, grabbed a dog and threw him to the front of the plane so hard that he hit the pilot.

And he immediately ran back to me.

I threw another, then another, then another, every time hitting the pilot, who was swearing at me and screaming at the dogs as we took off. I would keep throwing frantically, and I'd gain a little, with three or four dogs in the front. But they would always run back.

By now we were over open water in the Bering Sea and I had visions of the plane—which seemed to be barely wallowing through the sky—stalling and sinking into the waves and taking us all with it. I renewed my efforts, throwing dog after dog on top of dog beneath dog over dog, and they would run back, and I would imagine the plane settling into the water and would throw harder still.

I was still wearing my full winter gear, which included a down parka, and the dogs bit me and the pilot and ripped my parka so that soon the plane was filled with small white feathers and flying dogs and swear words and blood.

It took just twenty minutes to fly to Nome, and every one of those minutes I was sure we were going down into the water. I kept throwing dogs. Later I figured I threw a dog every five seconds, which is twelve a minute, so that in twenty minutes I threw 240 fifty-pound sled dogs fifteen feet—the length of the plane. When we landed at last in Nome, the pilot had two men put a cart under the tail, because it dropped to the ground and dragged as soon as our airspeed decreased.

He charged me eight hundred dollars for a twenty-minute flight and I started to complain until I looked at him and the inside of his plane and decided I was lucky it wasn't more.

I learned to fly when I got out of the army.

I was honorably discharged in May of 1962, my term having been extended to fight a war with Cuba, which never happened. While I didn't like the army at all, I did fall in love with flying while I was in uniform. Before I enlisted I had been on only one airplane ride in my life, when I was nine and a half and returning from the Philippines. When I enlisted in the army I went to basic training in Colorado by troop train and didn't get to fly then. But after I attended demonstrations of small fixed-wing aircraft at Fort Sill, Oklahoma, and Fort Bliss, Texas, I knew I wanted to learn to fly. I probably would have pursued it in the army—in fact, I took the physical and written tests for helicopter school—but I disliked the military so much that I waited until I was out.

When I was discharged I went to work in California in the aerospace field, at a lab at the China Lake Naval Ordnance Test Station. Within a week I'd signed up for lessons at a nearby airport.

GUTS

I started out in a small Aeronca Champ, a two-seater with one seat behind the other. The instructor's name was Joe and he sat in back and we took off and I will never forget the movement when the wheels first broke free of the runway and the plane slid a bit to the side. It was an incredible feeling of freedom, as if the earth no longer held me, and I knew then I was doomed, doomed to always love flying.

I kept up the lessons and soloed in the Aeronca, but with the freedom of flight came additional knowledge—that flying was very expensive. I made a decision then that was foolish and that I have regretted ever since: I had wasted so much time in the army, had fallen so far behind in my life (I thought), that if I was to support a family and have a career in aerospace engineering I could not spend the time and money it would take to get my pilot's license. So I stopped. I would take it up again, now that I have more time and some money, but my heart has gone bad and I wouldn't be able to get a license because of my health.

But I had soloed, I had learned to fly, and the knowledge stayed with me and became part of Brian when I put him in the plane and made him fly.

CHAPTER 2

MOOSE ATTACKS

. . . he saw a brown wall of fur detach itself from the forest to his rear and come down on him like a runaway truck. He just had time to see that it was a moose . . . when it hit him. HATCHET

I have spent an inordinate amount of time in wilderness woods, much of it in northern Minnesota, some in Canada and some in the Alaskan wilds. I have hunted and trapped and fished and have been exposed to almost all kinds of wilderness animals; I've had bear come at me, been stalked by a mountain lion, been bitten by snakes and punctured by porcupines and torn by foxes and once pecked by an attacking raven, but I have never seen anything rivaling the madness that seems to infect a large portion of the moose family.

I first witnessed this insanity when I was twelve, in northern Minnesota. I had just started hunting with a rifle. Back then there were none of today's modern hunting weapons and I was, to put it mildly, financially disadvantaged. I worked hard at setting pins in a bowling alley, selling newspapers in bars at night and laboring on farms in the summer (hoeing sugar beets for eleven dollars an acre and picking potatoes for five cents a bushel) to make enough money to buy clothing and supplies for school. There was little left for fancy weapons, and after saving for a long time I finally managed to come up with enough money for a Remington single-shot .22 rifle. It was bolt action, with a twist safety on the rear of the bolt, and had to be loaded for each shot by opening the bolt, which extracted the empty shell if you had just fired. Then you put a new cartridge into the chamber by hand, closed the bolt and fired. It was a long process and the end result was that it forced the shooter to pay attention to his first shot and make certain it was accurately placed. It also made the hunter careful not to waste his shot. Within a short time I was very accurate with this little rifle and was steadily bringing home rabbits and ruffed grouse, which I cleaned and cooked.

Just as they do today, game wardens had a great deal of say in how game laws were enforced, and if a family was poor or there were other special conditions, the wardens would sometimes overlook minor infractions. The legal hunting seasons were in fall and winter, but sometimes I hunted in spring as well, and it gave me food at times when my parents were on long drunks and didn't keep the re-frigerator filled. I would like to thank those game wardens who looked the other way now and then when they saw a scruffy kid come out of the woods with a not-quite-legal grouse or rabbit hanging on his belt.

Before I acquired that rifle, I had hunted a great deal with a bow, but on the day of my first moose incident I had been out with the rifle only a few times. It was early spring in the north woods of Minnesota, not far from the Canadian border, and I had seen many rabbits but hadn't shot any. I wanted grouse because I liked the taste of them fried in bat-ter, especially in spring, when they have been living on frozen high-bush cranberries all winter and have a crisp taste they lose in summer.

There was still snow in patches, and I was studying a large plot of old snow filled with budding willows because grouse like to hide in willows, when I heard something that sounded like a train about to run me down.

There was a kind of *bleeeeekkkk*, hoarse and very loud, coming from directly behind me and accompanied by a crashing in the brush, and I turned, raising my rifle (about as useful as a BB gun in these circumstances but we use what we have), to see two glaring red eyes coming at me at what seemed like sixty or seventy miles an hour.

I had hunted in these woods for several years and I had never seen a moose or even a moose track. I had heard of them, of course, and seen pictures of them. But there were very few left in Minnesota because they had been hunted out, so I had always dreamed of hunting moose up in Canada.

At the first instant I didn't realize that it was a large bull moose. He'd lost the previous year's antlers and hadn't grown new ones yet.

I just saw brown. I saw big. I saw death coming at me, snorting and thundering. I think I may have thought of phantoms, wood spirits, wild monsters—I most certainly did not think of moose.

I wish I could say that with cool precision I raised my trusty little .22 rifle and deftly protected myself. The truth is (and I would never again do this when confronting a moose) that I closed my eyes and waited to get hit. It had come so fast, the snorting, the crashing, the huge whatever it was, that I couldn't move, couldn't do anything except close my eyes.

A second passed, then another, and I opened one eye to see him pass me not three feet away. He had to be nearly seven feet tall at the hump. This move would have done credit to a pass in a bullfight. I knew then what he was and I fell back away from him. But the truth was that (a) he was a moose and (b) he was therefore insane, so at this time he hadn't the slightest interest in me. His target was something else.

Immediately behind me was a pine tree not more than six feet tall. It looked no different than other small pine trees, cute and well formed, like a little Christmas tree, but in that bull's mind maybe the tree had done something to insult him, or gotten in his way, or called him out, because he absolutely destroyed that tree.

Meanwhile, I scrabbled away into the willows on my back and then re-aimed my rifle, just in case—as if it would have helped to stop him. But he couldn't have cared less about me. He stomped and ripped and tore at that tree until it was broken off at the ground, and still he didn't stop until he had used his front hooves to break it into pieces (a method a cow moose would later try to use on me) and then shattered those into little more than splinters. Then he snorted, urinated on his work and walked off into the trees, leaving me to gasp (I had been holding my breath the whole time) and feel a strange pity for the tree.

I have since read that there is a kind of parasite that moose can pick up from eating in the water (they love water-lily roots) that attacks the brain and can cause madness. I wouldn't know about that, but not a year later I had another experience. I was sitting in a 1938 Ford truck with a farmer I was working for that summer. He had just stopped to roll a Bull Durham cigarette.

We had just passed through some woods that bordered a field where he wanted me to pick up rocks. Of all farm work, I hated this the most; every spring the frost pushed rocks up through the soil and they had to be gathered by hand and thrown on a skid behind a tractor, then dumped in a large pile in a fence corner. I dreaded the work but he was paying me the huge wage of five dollars a day plus room and board so I was glad of the job.

The road to the field was little more than an old logging trail through a thick stand of small poplars. The farmer had just finished rolling the cigarette and was snapping a match with his thumb to light it when a bull moose came out of the woods directly in front of us. He looked away, then at us, then raised all the hair on his hump (a signal I would later come to dread) and charged head-on into the truck.

"What in—"

I'm not certain what the farmer would have said next because he didn't have time to finish the sentence. The truck slammed backward and the moose backed off, lowered his head and hit the truck again, and again, and again, until we had been pushed back a good thirty feet. The grille was smashed into the radiator, which ruptured it and made the water boil out in a cloud of steam. The farmer used words I would not hear again until I enlisted in the army. Then the moose snorted and walked off and we had to walk four miles back to the farm and get a tractor to pull the truck home. It took weeks for us to repair it.

There seems to be a river of rage just below the surface in moose that has no basis in logic, or at least any logic that I can see.

Other times, when an attacking moose could easily have killed me, the creature just turned away and stopped charging. It's as if it had a sudden burst of good humor.

I was in a canoe once in summer, working my way along the side of a lake, angling for sunfish with a light rod and line, when I came around a bend in the lake and saw a moose with her head under water. I smiled because she looked so comical. Moose frequently nuzzle around lily-pad roots and they look silly, almost as if they intend to be funny and come up with leaves and roots hanging over their heads or mud streaming down their faces.

I had taken a stroke with the paddle just as I saw her, and while I was smiling the canoe drifted close to her—not four feet away. She raised her head, dripping with water and mud, and before I could even take the smile off my face she raised one enormous front hoof, put it on the gunwale of the canoe and pushed down as hard as she could.

The canoe did an instant and perfect barrel roll. One second I was sitting there and the next I—and all my gear—was in the water beneath the canoe, rod still in my hand, eyes wide open. With blurry vision I saw moose legs right in front of me and I turned and scrabbled/swam/dragged myself a few feet away and blew to the surface. I thought she would continue the attack and drive me into the mud on the bottom. But no. She decided to play with the canoe. The canoe had shipped a bit of water but it had rolled upright. With great deliberation, the moose reached out with a giant cloven hoof, put it on the side of the canoe and spun it again. Three times.

She watched it spin until it finally didn't come right side up again but lay overturned like a green log, and with that, apparently bored, she turned away. I was still standing there in four feet of water and mud. She walked off to eat lily-pad roots while I tried to find my tackle box and cooler and paddle. It had all been a joke.

I would not learn how truly serious a moose attack could be until I was in Alaska training for my first Iditarod.

Alaska was more than just a new and beautiful place to me. I grew up hunting and fishing in the north woods of Minnesota, and also spent time in the Colorado Rockies, the Wyoming Bighorns and the wilderness of south central Canada (where *Hatchet* takes place). But none of it had prepared me for the vastness, for the stunning size and beauty of the bush in Alaska.

And none of it had prepared me for the difference in moose—either in size or temperament. A fellow and I took my dogs up from Minnesota in an old truck, driving on the Alaska Highway for eight full days, and got to a place north of a trading post named Trapper Creek. I moved farther back into the woods and set up a winter camp. This was on a cold dark night in December three months before the race.

I went to sleep in an old vehicle used for a shelter. That first night I had dreams that could have been written by Jack London and edited by Robert Service, filled with prospectors and trappers and dogs named Fang and wild storms and cold so deep it froze the eyes out of men. (All of these things, except for a dog named Fang, later came to pass for me.) I was deep in this dream world when a scream tore me awake. It was a mix of terror and pain—I will never forget it—and I ran outside, barefoot, in my long underwear and my headlamp. (It was pitch dark around the clock except for about an hour and a half of grayness in the afternoon.) I was standing in four feet of snow with my light sweeping back and forth before I was quite awake.

I knew only one thing. It was a terrible scream and it had come from one of my dogs. They were tethered back in some spruce trees, out of the wind, and at first I could see nothing but shaking limbs and flying snow. Then came more screams—mixed with growls, snarls and the snapping of teeth— and I moved through the snow unaware of the cold, though I was barefoot and my feet would suffer for days after. Now I could see into the trees. And there was a cow—four, five hundred pounds of cow, and she was intent on killing my dogs.

I went insane. I didn't have a weapon, but I grabbed the small ax I used for chopping up frozen meat and stormed in after the moose, screaming and cursing louder than the dogs, swinging like a madman, the ax slashing back and forth, and I think the noise startled her or confused her. Whatever the reason, she turned as if to attack me, stomped on one more dog, then vanished into the night.

At first I thought she had killed two dogs and perhaps wounded two others. I gave what first aid I could, then ran to get dressed and harness up a team to carry the victims to the highway, where I could call a veterinarian from a pay phone.

I was wrong. No dogs died, though one had

a broken leg and another a cracked rib and both were out of the race for the season.

After that incident I borrowed a rifle.

Though I was attacked or had dangerous encounters many more times, none of my dogs ever got killed by moose, though I knew of other racers who lost dogs that way, either in training or during the race. But other dogs got injured in what I came to think of as passing attacks. They would develop in this way: We would be moving down a trail in the half-light and off to the side there would be a moose. This was a common occurrence. As a matter of fact, in a single training run lasting eight or ten hours it was usual to see eight or ten moose, always off to the side, always standing. Most of them would simply stand and stare as we went by. But on each run one or two would start trotting alongside the team.

This still didn't mean they were going to

attack. But it brought my attention to an absolute peak, and since the moose were faster than the dogs, with legs that seemed to go on forever, they were very much in control.

I learned to watch their backs. When the hair rose on their shoulders—not unlike the coat of an angry dog—it meant they were probably going to charge, and then I had to watch the head to see where the point of attack would be. If they aimed at the center of the team, the dogs would move out, there would be a scramble and we would get past, usually without much damage. If the moose aimed at the leaders I would yell at the dogs, turn them about and head back down the trail and away. This took some time and could end in possible injury to the dogs.

Quite often the moose would not even look at the dogs but would swing its head to stare at the sled and its eyes would go red and I would scream at the dogs to hurry, and grab the ax tied to the sled and either dodge or fight my way out.

Every dog run was interesting, many were frightening and on some I got injured. The worst attack, one I remembered when writing about Brian's difficulties with moose, came in the dark and caught me completely by surprise.

It was—and I've always wanted to use this phrase in a book—a dark and stormy night. *Dark* in the rest of the world means night but *dark* in the middle of a snowstorm in the bush of Alaska is very much, I think, what it would be like to be inside a cow.

I could see almost nothing. Of course I was wearing a headlamp and had batteries to spare but I had found that the dogs (like cats) could see quite well in the dark and the light made strange shadows that caused them to trip and stumble. So we were running in the dark and had gone about forty miles and were moving through a particularly thick stretch of spruce trees and I kept hearing a rattle in the sled. I was carrying a metal Thermos full of hot tea and it was bouncing against something, making a noise that was beginning to irritate me, so, standing on the back of the sled, I reached forward and down to adjust the Thermos.

At that precise moment a cow moose that had been standing in the darkened spruce trees swept me off the sled. I had no idea she was there, absolutely no warning that anything was coming, and the dogs hadn't seen or smelled her, or if they had, they didn't give any indication.

Suddenly I was upside down in the snow, flat on my back, and something enormous was stomping on me. Without any doubt, she was trying to kill me. I had been attacked many times, in brushing, passing attacks, but this one wanted me dead.

I quickly realized it was a moose, and as another dog driver had advised, I rolled into a ball and covered my head with my arms, presenting my back.

She completely worked me over. I didn't count the kicks and stomps but there were dozens. She stopped after a bit and I peeked at her, outlined against the snow, and she was staring at me, listening for my breath, and when at last I could hold it no longer and had to breathe again she heard it and renewed the attack.

I don't know how long she kept after me. It seemed hours, days. I lay as still as possible, trying to hide my breathing, but she kept coming back until *I* thought I was dead—and then she backed off. Thinking she was gone, I tried a small move, but she jumped me again. Finally I think she was convinced I was finished and she moved off into the forest.

I was spitting blood. Later I found that I had a cracked rib and two broken back teeth.

I had a gun—not on me, but on the sled. It was one of the few times I had brought a weapon on a run. A friend had loaned me a handgun, a .44 Magnum. The dogs had gone a hundred yards or so up the trail and stopped, tangled around a tree. I crawled, stumbled, fell to the sled and found the gun and turned and thought I would hunt her down, even if it took all my life. I wanted to kill her—six, seven times.

I know she was an animal. And that we are supposedly superior to animals (though I doubt we are *much* superior.) I understand all that. I know we are supposed to temper judgment with wisdom and logic. But in all honesty if somebody came to me now as I was sitting at my computer and said they had found that moose and I would only have to walk seven or eight hundred miles to get her, I would grab a rifle and go for it.

She made it personal, as the moose that went after Brian made it personal.

CHAPTER 3

THINGS THAT HURT

He had come through the crash but the insects were not possible. He coughed them up, spat them out, sneezed them out, closed his eyes and kept brushing his face, slapping and crushing them by the dozens, by the hundreds. HATCHET

I am living now on a sailboat in the Pacific Ocean and it is grand and beautiful and challenging and full of mystery and, sometimes, deadly. The woods where I hunted and trapped, camped and fished, grew and learned, are exactly the same. You can die out there. People die out there all the time—I have found their bodies and observed the damage done to them.

We have grown away from knowledge, away from knowing what something is really like, toward knowing only what somebody else *says* it is like. There seems to be a desire to ignore the truth in favor of drama.

Most people have heard of bear attacks, and we may know about moose attacks and wolf attacks (some rumors of which I believe are true, having seen wolves kill), but the truth is that more people are killed in North America by white-tailed deer and mule deer than by any other animal. Not just hurt, not just bruised or pushed or bumped, but killed. Most of them are killed in car accidents involving deer, but a goodly number are killed by direct attacks, especially in parks or other areas where wild deer have become used to people and beg for food. Many years ago I saw a small boy who couldn't have been four years old killed by a white-tailed buck in a state park.

It was not a petting zoo, but several half-tame deer would wander among the tourists, who fed them candy. It was early summer and a young buck—he had only a forked horn, still in velvet—had attached himself to the child and his mother. The child was eating those little white mints with the Xs across the surface. He gave one to the deer, and the buck took it gently enough and for some strange reason liked it. I was also young—about fourteen—and though I had hunted and killed deer by then, I viewed this buck as cute and a pet and not something to hunt, not something wild. I didn't understand when he stamped his feet in irritation if the child took too long to hand him another mint, didn't understand that it was a warning.

The deer ate four or five mints. The boy's mother had a camera and had backed away to get a better shot.

"Hold the candy away from him," she told her child. "Make him reach for it so I can get a picture. . . ."

The child took a mint from the package and held it out to the deer, which reached forward to take it; then the child pulled it back. The deer lashed out with his front hooves—two slashing jabs so fast, so incredibly fast, that the only thing I would see in my life to compete with it was a rattlesnake strike. I did not see motion. Just the boy standing there; then he was down and his chest and stomach were turning red where the buck's hooves had stabbed him. There was nothing, not a thing that all the dozens of people standing around could do. The strike with razor-sharp hooves was so lethal that even now, looking back, it is hard to believe. The pointed ends of the hooves were like small spears; they were in and out and had killed the little boy before anybody could move.

I can still see all this so clearly, and then there are only images: the mother with the camera half down, mouth open, eyes just beginning to show horror; the crowd of tourists, one man with popcorn halfway to his mouth, another lighting a cigarette, the match burning, glowing; all eyes on the deer, the small deer with blood on his hooves and forelegs, stamping his feet in anger, and finally the little boy, still and so small, lying on the gravel pathway, not terribly far from a sign that said Don't Feed the Deer.

Mosquitoes.

Hatchet shows how Brian had to deal with mosquitoes, and many of the letters I have received ask if they can really be that bad.

Of all the creatures on earth the mosquito is far and away the most deadly to man. Thousands of people die each year from many different strains of malaria or dengue fever. Whole populations have been wiped out by these two diseases—and they are both transmitted by the bite of mosquitoes.

When you consider that only half of all mosquitoes bite—only the female feeds on blood—these numbers are even more remarkable. One female mosquito can infect and possibly kill several people by biting someone with malaria or dengue fever and then spreading the disease by biting others. The death rate over the years is simply staggering, and when you consider that the spread of these killers is kept in check only with the most strenuous effort, which is never fully successful, Brian's plight becomes more understandable.

GUTS

Of course Brian was in the North, where there is no malaria and the mosquitoes tend not to spread disease, but the risks from infected bites are very real, and mosquitoes are more numerous in the North than they are in the Tropics. I have a theory that because the summers are so short, the northern mosquitoes are particularly vicious; they have very little time to hunt, feed, lay their eggs in water and repeat the cycle before the onset of winter, so the ones that attack efficiently and survive then reproduce their genes in the northern mosquito population.

There are many stories of how bad these mosquitoes can be. I have heard of small animals—rabbits, raccoons, even coyotes and fawn deer—that died from loss of blood. I haven't seen it personally but I believe the sources. I *have* seen workhorses so covered with mosquitoes that it was impossible to see the horse's coat, and deer temporarily blinded by swarms of mosquitoes. One summer I saw a rabbit that seemed close to death, lying still on the ground, its ears packed full of mosquitoes. I have suffered mosquitoes much worse than did Brian in *Hatchet*.

There was the incident in the sled dog kennel at our home in Minnesota. One summer night, I heard my dogs start barking. A bear had been bothering the dogs and had killed one of them, so I took a rifle and my headlamp and battery pack and ran out to the kennel in my underwear. At first I didn't see the bear but I thought I heard it, and I went deeper into the kennel without thinking.

The dogs were coated with repellent twice a week, so the mosquitoes didn't bother them, but the insects were still drawn to the dogs' exhaled breath—it is carbon dioxide that attracts them—and within seconds I realized that I had made a terrible mistake. I was standing in my underwear amid several dozen dogs on a warm summer night in the north woods, and to compound the error I was wearing a bright light on my head.

I must have attracted every mosquito in the county. The cloud swarmed over me, filled my nostrils and my eyes, flooded my mouth when I breathed. They blinded me, choked me and, worst of all, tore into me like eight or nine thousand starving vampires. I don't know how much blood I lost but I do know that when I regained the house—after a wild, blind run through two hundred yards of dark woods— there wasn't a square inch on my body that hadn't been bitten. I itched for a week.

The same thing happened to Brian, every night, until he discovered that smoke from a smoldering fire keeps mosquitoes away. And if that had been all Brian had to cope with it would have been bad enough. Bear attacks, moose attacks, deer attacks and hordes of mosquitoes would be more than most people could handle.

But in truth I was being kind to Brian. He didn't have to face blackflies, which bite and drink blood; horseflies, which bite and take out chunks of flesh; deerflies, which eat meat; wood ticks, which drink blood; midges, gnats, fleas, ants, spiders, centipedes and bees or wasps (fatal if a person is allergic), and consider that *all* of these can be attacking *all* the time, and further add in the chance of infection . . .

Survival in the woods almost seems impossible.

I was canoeing once on a river in late summer with another man. We were working downstream on a wild river in northern Minnesota, setting off on a six-day run to lay out a trapline to work with in the fall and winter, and we came to a place where the sun was particularly hot and a large hatch of deerflies had developed.

We had (I thought) adequate repellent and we kept going. But there seemed to be more flies and still more flies, biting right through the repellent, and I looked up and realized that they were so thick I could not see the man sitting at the other end of the canoe, just fourteen or so feet away. They went after my eyes and then his eyes, and I dimly made out that he was waving a paddle in the air, as if swatting them, and swearing and yelling, and I tried to do likewise, and we unbalanced the canoe and flipped it. All our gear went in the water with us. Foolishly, we had not tied our equipment into the canoe, so it fell out as we went over.

I grabbed for my pack and held it—easy because I was in the rear and the pack was right in front of me. The guy in the front of the canoe could not reach around in time and his pack went to the bottom because he had filled it with canned goods. We never did find it, or the .22 single-shot rifle or our cooking gear or our cartridges. We set up a quick camp there onshore and dived into the muddy water, but there was a good current and even allowing for drift and working in search grids, searching downriver did no good. We lost all the gear except for matches and some potatoes in my pack, and in the next five days, working the rest of the way downriver, we got to apply a lot of the skills that Brian learned in *Hatchet*, such as spearing fish and making bows and willow arrows to shoot grouse.

In the wilderness, it's simply amazing how often a small thing can almost instantly snowball into a life-threatening disaster.

At one time in my life I shot muzzle-loading rifles a great deal and went to many of the tournaments and shoots around the country. I never got into the reenacting thing that so many do—wearing buckskins and pretending to live the way they imagine the old mountain men lived—but when I started to write the Tucket Adventures series I researched that era, thinking that of all the people who live in an extreme manner the mountain men must have been the most radical. They'd head off with nothing but a horse and rifle and seemingly ride into legend. Jim Bridger, Kit Carson—wild men and wild country.

But my research revealed something else. There were quite a few men who thought they could head into the mountains and get rich from fur trapping. But most died in the first year. The big killer wasn't bear attacks, or Indian attacks, or mountain-lion attacks—which I'm afraid most sources talk about. Those things sometimes happened, and I wrote about them in the Tucket Adventures, but most of the men died of malnutrition, or more specifically, dysentery brought on by malnutrition. Some studies indicate that as many as eighty percent of the so-called mountain men died in their first year in the wild, just from eating the wrong food or not knowing that they had to eat something other than meat.

The point, and here is something I learned slowly and sometimes the hard way, is that it often seems that everything in the wilderness is conspiring to harm you in one way or the other, and this can lead to almost absurd occurrences. I know of a man who was killed by poison ivy—he had an allergic reaction to it while on a fishing trip and died in the boat while they were rushing him across a lake to a small town where there was a doctor.

The solution to facing all these dangers, a

solution that came very rapidly to me and to Brian, is knowledge. It can come from anywhere; from reading, from listening to people or from personal experience. However it comes, the knowledge must be there.

CHAPTER 4

Killing to Live: Hunting and Fishing with Primitive Weapons

He had sat a whole night and shaped the limbs carefully until the bow looked beautiful. Then he had spent two days making arrows. The shafts were willow, straight and with the bark peeled, and he fire-hardened the points and split a couple of them to make forked points. HATCHET

I can remember the first game I ever shot with a rifle. I had bought a .22 caliber single-shot rifle. It was a Remington with a rotating safety on the rear of the bolt, and the bullets cost eighteen cents a box for long-rifle cartridges. They were called Federals and had lead-colored bullets instead of the copper-colored ones that came years later. I bought the shells at Nelson's grocery and then rode on my Hiawatha bike seven miles out of town to an area filled with small swamps and stands of poplar. It was fall and the big flocks of ducks and geese had started to fly south. I also knew that there were grouse in the poplars and thought I might have some luck there. I pedaled along until I saw some ducks off in a field full of shallow water. The day was sunny but it had rained hard the day before. I laid the bike down in a ditch at the side of the country road. I took a shell from my pocket and put it in the rifle, making certain it was on safety. Then I crept along in the ditch on the side away from the ducks until I was opposite where they were swimming. I peeked over the edge for one quick look, then pulled back. There were four mallard ducks about thirty yards away— three on the left and one on the right. The three were hens, plain colored and drab, and the other, set off three feet, was a drake. I twisted the rifle off safety and crept up to the edge of the ditch again, brought the rifle to my shoulder and slid the barrel out through the low grass in front of me. I aligned the small bead of the front sight in the dimpled notch of the back, then set the bead on the body of the drake and squeezed the trigger. There was a large splash—I did not hear the rifle fire—and a short second or two of flopping. The three hens took off, bursting vertically with the sound of the shot, but the mallard drake lay there, still, dead. I ran across the water and mud and grabbed him and held him up and carried him home and plucked him and baked him in the oven and ate most of him that night.

It was all wrong, of course, and illegal and very unsporting. To use a rifle on a duck, to shoot it sitting. All wrong. I would hunt ducks many more times, with a single-barrel

12-gauge shotgun, and I would shoot them
flying with No. 4 shot, and I would remember
some of them, many of them.

But not like the first one. I recall every aspect of that hunt with clarity and detail—the
colors of the leaves, the temperature of the
air, the soft cold wind riffling the water—and
I point it out not because it had a specific
bearing on how Brian lived in *Hatchet* (he did
not, after all, use the rifle even when he found
it) so much as to show how incredibly important hunting was for me when I was young,
when I was Brian's age.

Hunting virtually became my life—sometimes with other boys, though few of them
seemed as devoted as I was to it, but more
often alone. Hunting, along with fishing, was
all I lived and breathed for, all I was or
wanted to be.

At that time I lived in a small town in northern Minnesota near the edge of the bush—un-trackable miles of wilderness—and everything in my life phased into hunting or fishing. Every day when school let out, after I finished my work selling newspapers, I made for the woods near town. On Friday nights I set pins for the bowling league; after closing then, at eleven, I would sometimes take off on my bike and pedal out of town and set up camp near the river that flowed out of the wilderness and through town so that I could get an early start on the weekend hunting or fishing.

The wilderness pulled at me—still does—in a way that at first baffled me and then became a wonder for me. I never thought of where that river went after it passed through town—down to where it joined the Missis-sippi, I supposed, and then through other towns and cities and gone; I really didn't care. But where it came *from*—that was all that mattered. Somewhere north, somewhere in the woods, somewhere *wild*—that's all I cared about, all I wanted to see, to know.

I hunted a great deal with rifles and shotguns and I trapped and snared animals for a living. There are people who say that is wrong, and perhaps they are right—though virtually nothing in nature dies of old age except man and I'm not sure of the morality or immorality of their claim or why it is better for a coyote to kill a rabbit than it is for a man who will also eat the rabbit—but these questions did not exist then for most people. Trapping was considered an honorable way to make a living and those of us who could live from the woods did so. We could sell snowshoe rabbits (called snowshoes because of their large feet, which enabled them to run on top of the snow) for ten cents each. This sounds like a paltry amount but it was possible to take twenty rabbits a day with stovepipe-wire snares (there were thousands upon thousands of rabbits), and two dollars a day in those days was as much as I made working on farms in the summer; men worked in factories for only eight dollars a day. So the two dollars went a long way toward buying school clothes or food, and though this experience of mine didn't point directly to Brian, it led that way. What I learned trapping and killing game was how to see things: how to look for a line, for a curve where there shouldn't be a curve, for movement where nothing should move, and these things became useful, became life-savers for Brian.

But I soon became disenchanted with firearms. I continued to use them when hunting because they provide a very efficient way to get wild meat for the table and it was important to have the meat. In most respects, when used correctly, firearms are a humane way to kill an animal—more humane certainly than nature, which can be astonishingly slow and cruel when it comes to death. One needs only to watch a wolf kill a deer to know this.

But the *noise*! There is nothing worse than what the sound of a gun does to the woods. One second there is the wonderful almost-silence of the forest—birds, rustles of leaves, soft sighs of wind in the pines—and the next instant there is the crashing crack, worse than thunder, alien to everything that is in the woods, harsh and cutting and loud, and warning everything within a mile that you are there.

Terrible. Even from the first, using only the .22, which has a small sound compared with shotguns or high-velocity, big-bore rifles, I did not like the disruption that came with firing a weapon. Everything stops. All sounds and movement cease—it's as if the noise of the rifle kills the whole woods. And it does not return to normal for a long time. If you are hunting small game, rabbits for instance, and shoot fairly often, the woods never have time to return to a normal state. Everything from small birds to large game is in a constant panic. Consequently, if you hunt with a firearm it's possible to be successful, to take a lot of game and kill it humanely, yet never know what the woods are really like, how animals move, why they do what they do or when they do it.

With a bow there is silence, or near silence—only the soft twang of the string when released—and all the purity of the forest remains. And here is perhaps one of the great paradoxes of hunting. If the hunter is very good and uses modern equipment—some of the new broadheads are truly deadly—the kill can be efficient and relatively fast. But it cannot be as fast as a rifle because an arrow lacks what the military calls the hydraulic shock of impact that a bullet has when it hits flesh. Unless the arrow is almost perfectly placed, it can be a very slow death indeed for the animal.

Still, early in my hunting life I decided that I would rather hunt with a bow than a rifle. Luckily for Brian, I started using a bow well before the advent of all the modern technology that has embraced archery (and everything else, for that matter); compound bows were still a quarter of a century in the future and even laminate bows of modern materials—fiberglass and wood strips—were only beginning to come on the market. Fred Bear was just starting his company and the first so-called modern bow that I bought was a Bear Cub of forty pounds pull. Forty pounds was the minimum legal pull-weight for large game in Minnesota although deer had been killed with much lighter bows. It is generally acknowledged that the weight of the bow is not as important as the sharpness of the broadhead on the arrow.

When I started to hunt with a bow I could not afford to buy one. Even a Bear Cub model was more than thirty dollars, almost a full week's wage for a man working at an adult job. Setting pins at the bowling alley, I made seven cents a line, and if I worked two lanes I might make four lines an hour—twenty-eight cents. To get a bow I would have had to set pins for more than a hundred hours and not used the money for clothes or food or school supplies.

And so I made my first real hunting bow. I wasn't limited to the primitive methods that Brian was because I had much better tools available at a neighbor's wood shop, but the results were not too far removed from what Brian achieved. There was a famous archer named Howard Hill back then. He was incredible, doing things like hitting quarters in the air, shooting two arrows into a target so that the second arrow split the first—and hunting. The man was a hunting maniac. He hunted all the great game of the world, taking elephants, rhinos, bears, lions—everything. A lot of what he did was show-offy stuff, but he brought many young people to archery and tried to make it widely accessible by publishing pamphlets on how to make bows and arrows.

Hill swore by wood from lemon trees for his bows because he said it kept its spring best and would not "take a set," that is, stay bent when unstrung the way some other woods did. So I ordered a lemon-wood stave one and a half inches square with straight grain and no knots, which was just two dollars from the lumberyard. Following Howard Hill's instructions, I used a small hand plane and then pieces of broken beer bottles to shave the limbs into shape, finishing them with sandpaper, working down from coarse to very fine. I found an old tennis racket, unwrapped the leather handle and used that for the bow handle. I used a small rat-tail file to cut nocks—notches for the string—and prestretched nylon fish line, twisted on itself, became a bowstring. When I first strung it the bow was unbalanced, one limb bending more than the other, so I unstrung it, per Mr. Hill's instructions. I shaved a bit off the stiff limb, and kept working that way, stringing and unstringing the bow, until the limbs balanced. I never tested it accurately, but according to a crude fish scale the bow pulled between thirty-five and forty pounds at twenty-six inches of draw. That was a stout bow for a thirteen-year-old—what Brian would have called a war bow.

Arrows were a bit more of a problem. I tried making my own shafts out of pine dowels and they worked, but not well. For two dollars and some change I sent for a cheap little sheet-metal jig that would allow me to glue on three feathers at one time in a relatively straight fashion. Feathers came from a slaughterhouse near the edge of town. They were always killing chickens but now and then they would run turkeys through, and on one of those days I went down and pulled feathers from the right wings of turkeys (again, per Howard Hill) until I had several hundred. You must use all feathers from either the right or left wing because the feathers curve to cup the air, and the curve has to be consistent.

Of course the feathers don't come ready to use. Each feather has a wide side and a narrow side. The wide portion is the one you keep, and you process each feather by putting it between two pieces of wood and cutting off the narrow band with a razor, then sanding the round quill down flat so that it will glue well to the wooden shaft.

Then it is a simple matter to use a small rat-tail file to nock one end of the arrow for the string and (I learned after several broken shafts) to smear the nock with glue. This toughens it up so that the arrow can take the shock of the string's striking it without splitting.

The arrow point was a problem at first, and sometimes I just sharpened the wood and fire-hardened it the way some primitive tribes used to do it. But without a separate point, the shafts split easily when they hit hard dirt or rocks. They needed some metal to strengthen them, but I could not afford to buy points. However, I quickly found that the word *point* kept me from the real solution. When you use an arrow on small game, you don't want a pointed end but a blunt one. When a blunt strikes, it causes much more shock and a quicker kill. The blunt still goes through the animal, even though it's not sharp, and it has some knockdown potential. Then I found that used .38 Special cartridge cases from the pistol range out of town slipped perfectly over the shafts and made as good a blunt tip as any I could buy. There were plenty of empties there, so I quickly found enough to last years, and in a short time I was in the woods hunting small game.

I soon found there is a great deal of difference between hunting game with a home-made bow and actually killing game. There's a frustration index with arrows that you don't have with guns. If a gun is aimed correctly and held steady and the trigger squeezed correctly, the bullet will almost always strike where it is pointed. An arrow can be aimed correctly and held properly and released exactly right and still miss the target completely because of wind or a tiny branch sticking in the way or, apparently, just bad luck.

That first time I went out hunting with my new homemade lemon-wood bow, I had ten arrows, all with blunts. It was fall and the leaves were changing and there cannot be a more beautiful time to be in the woods. You walk through dappled color and streams of light and the air is crisp and clean, with none of the soft mugginess of summer, and I remember feeling as I still do when going into fall woods: Everything is new and out ahead of me and only good things can come.

I worked out along the river. I had a fried-egg sandwich wrapped in waxed paper (there were no zippered bags or plastic wrap then) and a boiled potato in a paper sack, both tucked into the pocket of my army-surplus field jacket. On my back I had a leather quiver made from an old leather jacket sleeve with a piece of shoe sole laced in for the bottom.

I had not gone a mile before I saw a grouse. It was sitting back in some willows, and I caught a slight movement of its head before it froze, or I never would have seen it. I worked in close, then closer, until I couldn't have been more than ten feet away. I raised the bow, drew the shaft, held for the outline of the bird and released.

The arrow snapped clean from the bow, followed my sight line down to the grouse and . . . missed—not by much, an inch to the right of the grouse, so close the shaft nearly rubbed it. Even with the blunt tip the arrow stuck in the soft ground and quivered. It didn't seem possible. But the grouse sat there, still, unmoving, not a feather different. I held my breath, slowly raised my arm back over my shoulder and took another arrow out of the quiver. Moving ever so slowly, I nocked another arrow; raised the bow; drew, using a solid three-finger hold on the string; held until I *knew* I couldn't miss, and released.

The arrow plowed into the ground slightly to the left of the grouse. The bird sat there, not moving, frozen, waiting.

Another arrow. Up. Draw. Hold. Release.

Miss.

Hmmm, I thought. This was not possible. The grouse still sat there. And if it seems unbelievable that a grouse would hold still for all this waving a bow around, arms over shoulders grabbing at arrows, bow-raising and hissing arrows, it must be remembered that grouse have evolved over millions of years to use the freeze defense, and it has worked against predators so well that they have it locked into their genes. At a much later date, I would see a grouse in a tree about eight feet off the ground and have time to cut a long stave with a hunting knife, carve one end into a needle point—all while the grouse watched—and spear the same grouse and have it for dinner. Once I took a grouse off the ground with my bare hands.

Still, this particular grouse was especially long-suffering. I pulled another arrow, raised the bow again, drew, released.

Missed.

With all ten arrows. They were around the bird like a cage and I simply could not believe it, could not believe that I could miss that many times from not ten feet away. It just wasn't possible.

I was out of arrows and the grouse was still there and I thought of using the bow like a club or maybe finding a rock—I certainly was never going to kill this bird with an arrow unless I walked up and stabbed it with one. Then I decided to reach forward carefully and pull one of my arrows out of the ground and use it over again. Later in my life this would work, but this time I wasn't that lucky.

I moved forward slowly.

It sat there, carved in stone.

Five feet away, then three—I could have just fallen on the bird and would have done that, except that I would have landed on all my arrows. So I crouched, leaned almost directly over the grouse and laid my hand on one of the arrows.

And a mass of feathers exploded into my face.

Anybody who has heard a grouse take off will never forget it. Along with its freeze defense it has evolved a takeoff that is, to say the least, startling. The wings cup air and beat at a tremendous rate, creating a concussive explosion so loud it sounds like an artillery round going off.

In this case, it was directly in my face. I

almost wet myself. Then I fell backward, nearly somersaulting as the grouse flew past where my head had been and vanished into the dappled leaves.

Clearly, I thought, I am doing something wrong.

I hunted all that first day and shot at several rabbits and two more grouse and missed them all. Then I decided to find out what I was doing wrong. I moved to a clearing in the woods and found a gopher mound with soft dirt that wouldn't hurt the arrows—I was down to eight now, having lost two that had snaked beneath the grass and disappeared—and put a leaf about the size of my palm in the dirt for a target and shot at it from about ten feet away.

And missed.

I kept trying, slamming away the dirt until at last I realized that if I simply looked at the leaf in general I would miss it. Sometimes I would come near it, but I would still miss. At that time almost nobody used a sight, unless you counted using the tip of your arrow as a kind of aiming point. Everybody shot by instinct, simply looking and "feeling" where the arrow would go, so there wasn't a distinct spot to aim at.

There had to be a better way. I started thinking of exactly where the tip of the arrow would go, not just in general terms but exactly in what spot. I did not look at the whole leaf but at the tiniest part of the center of the leaf and I imagined the arrow hitting there, right *there* where I was looking, in the center of the center of the leaf.

And I started to hit. Not the center, at least not always—although I think that is how it happens for truly gifted people such as Howard Hill and some of the trick shooters

GUTS

who travel around doing exhibitions now. I
think they *always* see the center of the center
and always hit that point.

But I hit the leaf. Usually at the edge, but
again and again. If I let my eye wander and
look at the leaf in general I would miss, but
when I concentrated I almost always hit, and
after practicing this until my fingers were
nearly bleeding through the finger tab on my
draw hand, I went back to hunting.

There was an immediate difference. I
hadn't gone thirty yards into the woods when
I saw a grouse. This one did not freeze. It flew
away, but for some reason it stopped on a
limb about thirty feet from me. This seemed
a bit far, but the tree was situated so that if I
tried to move closer I would be in thick brush
and unable to shoot straight up. I drew and
held and started to release and realized that I
was thinking of the grouse as a whole, not
focusing. I eased off, cleared my mind of

thoughts and aimed again, thinking of the very center of the grouse, and released and knew, *knew* that I would hit the bird.

The blunt took it almost in the center, driving it back and off the limb, to flop briefly and then to lie still. I moved through the brush to where the bird lay and saw the shaft, the blunt driven completely through as if it had been a sharp point and killing the grouse as fast as a rifle.

And here I found another advantage to using a bow. A rifle destroys flesh—again, because of hydraulic shock as the bullet passes through the tissue. Worse, if it first passes through the gut, it carries the contents of the gut into the meat and ruins still more.

An arrow, even a blunt, makes a simple hole and doesn't ruin any meat.

That night I cleaned and cooked the grouse over a fire and ate it, arrow hole and all. I hunted the rest of that weekend and took two rabbits and another grouse and they were all clean kills. I ate the meat the rest of that week, cooking it after school, and made more arrows.

Only this time I made broadheads. It was time to hunt bigger game.

There is as big a difference between hunting small game and hunting large game with a bow as there is between hunting small game with a bow and hunting it with a rifle.

First, of course, you cannot use blunts. With deer—or elk and moose, for that matter—the deadliness comes from the cutting power of the broadhead. This was known by primitive hunters as well as modern ones, and they used razor-sharp bits of stone or antler or flint to make a cutting edge that would do more damage as the arrow went through. The truth is, it is possible to kill with a simple pointed piece of wood—and probably all animals in the world, including elephants (or mastodons), have been killed in this manner—as long as it is very sharp and the point is placed exactly right, in the heart, for instance, or for a slower kill, in the lungs. But it is so much easier if there is a widened cutting edge involved.

And so, broadheads.

When I was young we were limited to simple two-bladed heads and the three-bladed. There were no razor-blade-type inserts as there were later, which would vastly improve the efficiency of the heads. The broadheads of the time came very dull and had to be sharpened, first with a file and then with a stone, honed until they could take hair off your arm.

I chose the three-bladed types for two reasons. First, they had an added cutting edge, which I thought was important, but perhaps more significant, they were army surplus (the military term was MA-3) and much cheaper. I understood they were used for "quiet" operations, although even when I was in the army and had knowledge of such things I could find no indication they had ever been used. Whatever the reason, they were available for just ten cents each and they were stout and well made (wouldn't break every time you missed and hit a tree limb), and while hard to sharpen they would hold a good edge once they were honed. (An aside: Last year for Christmas I was given a bronze arrowhead from about 300 B.C., and while it is smaller than the MA-3 head, it is so similar that I wondered if they didn't use the antique heads for a model.)

I bought a dozen MA-3s and made twelve big-game arrows using Port Orford cedar shafts I got for four cents each by mail order. I spent a huge amount of time on each arrow, making certain the feathers were perfectly straight and the head was truly aligned so that it wouldn't "plane" off to the side or fight the feathers for direction when released.

I had already killed a deer with a rifle—actually an old 16-gauge single-shot Browning shotgun with slugs—by the time I began to hunt with a bow, hunting with my farmer uncles in the fall. This was less hunting than it was gathering meat. Men with rifles were posted at clearings while boys and other men were sent to "drive" the woods through and push the deer out to be shot. It was not particularly sporting and was not meant to be. It was gathering meat for the family for winter. I was carrying a shotgun nearly longer than I was tall, staggering through swamp grass and snow up to my waist, when a buck jumped up in front of me and stood still, broadside to me. I raised the shotgun without thinking, cocked the hammer, and shot. The buck dropped, the big slug almost knocking him sideways. I, of course, got buck fever and stammered a yell for my uncle Gordy, who was pushing brush next to me, and he came over and helped me gut the buck and drag him out to the road so we could add him to the row of deer already taken by the posted men. It was my first deer, but it couldn't really be called hunting so much as just luck for me and panic by the deer, which stood forty feet away while a kid knocked him over with an old single-barrel scattergun and what they used to call a punkin-ball slug.

Hunting, true big-game hunting with a bow, is much more an art and much more demanding, and initially I wasn't sure how it should be done. Some people would simply find a deer trail and either hide in brush or get up in a tree and wait, on a "stand," until a deer came by. Others would put on soft moccasins and walk slowly, very slowly, through the woods, as quietly as possible, and walk up on feeding or bedded deer and get a shot at them before they were aware.

I initially decided to hunt by moving, I think more because as a young boy I wasn't patient enough to sit and wait. Later I favored the stand method, working from camouflage. And my first bow-killed deer was taken that way.

I was near an old abandoned homestead, long ago rotted to wreckage by the northern winters, and I saw a small buck walk behind the caved-in building. I waited a few seconds at full draw until he walked out. Everything worked as it was supposed to and I hit the deer just behind the shoulder—one of the blades of the broadhead actually cut the side of his heart—and he walked a few steps, and lay down, then curved his head back and died.

But it was my second kill of a deer with a bow that truly applies to Brian's hunting in *Hatchet*. Two years later, when I was fifteen, I was hunting and absolutely nothing was going right. Normally, fall in the north woods is a time of clear days and nights, crisp weather, wonderful bright sun and brilliant leaves. That year there was none of it. It rained—cold rain during the day, all day, a soft, gray drizzle that froze at night into a thin layer on the ground, too thin to hold weight, so that when you tried to walk on it you broke through into the cold mud, and everything, everything in the world had a cold, wet drabness that made even my fifteen-year-old bones ache.

It was, paradoxically, the best time to walk-hunt. The water kept the grass unbrittle, so it didn't crackle and make noise, and the water dripping from limbs covered the sound of walking. Years later I learned that storm fronts create the best conditions for hunting because game animals lie down and are not as wary as normal. It was the kind of hunting Brian would have to do—hunting when it wasn't necessarily pleasant to hunt; hunting because he had to, hunting to live.

About three one afternoon I came to the edge of a swamp that was absolutely covered with deer trails, many of them so fresh the water was still running into the hoof prints. The swamp presented a problem. I was wearing rubber boots, hardly the thing for quiet walking, although in that weather they weren't so loud, and my feet were still relatively dry and even retained a slight warmth. But the boots were only calf high and the water in the swamp was sure to be deeper than that. I would probably flood my boots.

But there were deer tracks all over the swamp.

And I did have matches to light a fire and there were plenty of dead birch trees around for tinder—birch bark is the quickest way to get a fire going in wet weather. If I got wet, I could dry out.

So I nocked an arrow to the string to be ready, stepped off into the swamp and found I had underestimated the difficulties.

On my first step I sank through the muck on top and both boots filled with cold, muddy water. I had been looking down on the swamp from a small hill but now that I was in it, I could see that the grass was much taller than I had originally thought. Once I had sunk into the mat beneath the vegetation, the grass was about four inches over my head and I was soon walking down a narrow almost-tunnel with water pouring into my boots. I could see only about four feet in front of me.

Nobody could call this hunting. Inside thirty yards I was simply trying to keep moving, and in another thirty I just wanted out. I won't say I panicked—I wasn't in any danger. But I was becoming intensely uncomfortable and most decidedly not in control of my situation and decided that if I didn't come to higher and drier ground in a very short time I would turn and go back.

I took one step, then heard the first strange sound.

There are many different aspects of sound in the woods. Birds sing; small things—usually sounding like very large things—scurry through the grass and underbrush and make rustling noises; sometimes heavy things crash down, maybe a dead limb at last falling off a rotten tree pulled apart by a bear looking for grubs or ants to eat.

But all the sounds have reason to them, a sense of belonging. There are only two things that stand out and cause the hair to go up on the back of your neck. One is a sudden silence; during day and night, during rain, even during snow, there is some sound, and when it quits it almost always means that something not good is happening. Perhaps a wolf is moving through, looking for something to kill, or a hawk or an owl is hunting over the place where you are standing. Recently I talked to a man who was attacked by a great white shark while diving and he said that just before he was hit, the ocean, which is usually deafening, grew strangely quiet. "I should have listened to the silence," he said, shaking his head. "I'd still have my right leg."

The second kind of auditory alert is sudden or very loud sound, and the combination of the two when it is completely unexpected can be a life-altering experience. I was once in a tent half-asleep when what I took to be a tree limb poked me through the tent material, and I angrily kicked out at it, only to find that I had just kicked a bear in the backside. It had leaned against the tent while smelling around the dead campfire for bits of food. The ensuing snort did wonders for waking me up and changing my whole attitude about kicking bear in the butt.

Now, in the swamp, I heard a great bounding noise, as if something large had jumped in the air and landed on the swamp grass just ahead of me.

And then, half a second later, another one, then another, all coming closer, straight at me.

All of this in about two seconds. Automatically, I raised the bow and drew the arrow back, until the back of the three-sided broadhead rested against the belly of the bow just over my hand.

Another bound.

All was in slow motion now. I had a fleeting thought that it had been raining hard and that the feathers on my arrow were wet. I wondered how it would affect the flight or accuracy of the shot. Then another bound and the grass in front of me parted, and coming at me, at a full run, was a twelve-point buck (six on each side, counted later), and I saw him, not ten feet away, just as he left the ground, and I released the arrow and saw it disappear into the center of his chest, just vanish into him. He was already in the air and hit by the arrow when he saw me and he couldn't change the direction of his jump but he tried and so instead of hitting me full on, he twisted in the air and hit me with his side as he fell over me.

It was like being hit by a truck. I went down, arrows and bow flying. One of his legs tangled in the bowstring and in the violent kicking to get loose he broke the bow and several arrows that had been tossed out of my quiver as I went over backward. (I was indeed very lucky not to have fallen on one of the broadheads, the fate a year earlier of a man I knew. He fell out of a tree-stand onto one of his own arrows; the broadhead cut the artery on the inside of his thigh and he bled to death before he could get help.)

In this case, other than being soaked and covered with mud, I was unharmed. The deer had been hit solidly. The arrow had driven into the center of his chest and slightly up, hitting the heart almost exactly in the middle. After colliding with me, he had continued over in a sideways somersault, bounded to his feet, taken two staggering steps, then settled, rather than fallen, in the grass.

I was a mess, with broken arrows and the bow in pieces, string wrapped around my head and the deer kicking his last. I had been told to always test a deer by poking it to make certain it was dead so that it couldn't kick you when you leaned over it. But as I rolled to my feet and moved toward the buck, my hunting knife in my hand, I saw that he was truly dead. His eyes were glazed and gone and he wasn't breathing. I felt the sadness that comes with killing when you hunt but also the elation that comes with having succeeded—it makes for an odd mixture of emotions. I gutted the carcass and cleaned it out with grass to keep the meat from rotting. Heat from the guts as they begin to decompose will cause this, even in hard winter, because the hair keeps the carcass warm and allows the internal organs to go off.

I had taken a very large buck—even dressed out he was close to two hundred pounds. At the time I weighed about a hundred and thirty. I was in the middle of a quagmire swamp two miles in from the road where I'd left my bicycle. And then it was four miles back to town.

I was to learn, as Brian learned later, that there is sometimes a huge difference between hunting and killing the animal and dealing with the results. I had to get the deer back to town, where I knew a butcher who would cut the carcass up into freezer-sized packages in exchange for a quarter of the meat.

I somehow horsed the buck out of the swamp; it took me well over an hour to go the short distance to higher, more solid ground. Once there I used the bowstring and my belt (I would never again hunt without a fifteen-foot piece of light rope in my pocket) to rig up a waist harness, which I looped through a hole in the buck's lower jaw, then around my waist, so that I could drag the dead deer to the highway.

Sounds simple, doesn't it? I mean, I knew it would be hard work but it sounds simple. I would just take my time and drag the deer to the highway, then tie him across the bicycle in some way and push him back to town.

Except that I was dragging an animal that weighed more than me and there was no snow to make the dragging easier.

It was a nightmare. I started dragging in midafternoon and I had not gone a mile when darkness caught me. With the dark came increased rain, and I was on the verge of making a wet, cold, very dreary camp. I didn't have a raincoat on, just an old canvas duck jacket that was semiwaterproof, and I was soon soaked and getting colder.

I stopped dragging the buck before hard dark and set up camp in some willows. Luckily I was on the edge of another small swamp—there were hundreds of them in this area—and I found some dead birch skirting the grass area. With my knife I cut bark from one of the dead trees and used it for kindling. Then I covered the bark with small pine twigs broken off from the underside of dead limbs that were still relatively dry. I had matches, of course. I would not go out without matches. I had waterproofed them with melted wax and I carried them in a waterproof case. I used one of them to start the birch bark and at length had a sputtering half-fire going. I added what partially dry wood I could find under trees, stacked more wet wood on top and soon had a good-sized blaze crackling away, which did much to bring my spirits up.

Of course I was starving, but I had plenty of meat. I cut strips of rib meat off the buck and cooked them, tallow and all, draped over the fire on green sticks (green so that they would not burn), and ate them when they were just short of burnt. They tasted—without salt or pepper or bread—incredibly fine and I must have eaten four or five pounds of meat before I was at last full, my mouth and tongue caked with venison tallow. Then I gathered all the wood I could find by firelight, until I had enough for several nights. I lay near the fire, dozing and adding wood all night.

The wolves came not too long after midnight, brought by the smell of blood and meat. I could see their eyes in the firelight, and for a few moments I was afraid and missed my bow terribly, but the fire kept them well away. They probably would not have bothered me, but I still had some broadheads, which I determined to use as hand spears if necessary. This comforted me.

The wolves left well before first light and when it was bright enough to see I went to work on the carcass. I skinned part of it down the side and used the raw skin to make a better harness than just the belt around my waist. After a meal of cooked rib meat and peaty-tasting water from a spring nearby, I set off dragging again.

I dragged until I couldn't stand it any longer, until every muscle in my body was on fire. Then I tried to haul the carcass in an over-the-shoulders fireman carry, but I only made about fifty yards before my legs buckled, so I stopped and took a break, building another fire and cooking some more rib meat. It actually occurred to me only half in jest that perhaps the best solution was just to stay out in the woods until I had cooked and eaten the whole deer. It was the weekend and my folks probably wouldn't miss me—they didn't know where I was half the time and would probably think I was staying at a friend's house. But at school, where I was mostly flunking, they would notice that I wasn't there.

So I had to get back, and I worked all that day, dragging and stopping, and finally, completely exhausted, I arrived at the road just short of dark. By then most of the hair was gone off one side of the carcass. My bicycle was still there and I lugged and pulled at the carcass until it was across the seat and the handlebars and started pushing it down the road. It was nearly impossible—the carcass kept falling off to one side or the other—but the wheels made it infinitely better than dragging. After a few hundred feet I worked out a balance point and it became slightly less difficult.

It was an almost-deserted back road but there were some farms out along the edge of the forest and I thought, or dreamed, or hoped and prayed, that somebody, anybody, would come along in a truck and give me a lift to town.

It did not happen. I wobbled and rolled down the road at about a mile an hour, stopping often to rub my legs, more often to get the deer back on the bike. It was well after midnight when I pulled into the driveway of the apartment. I found some rope and pulled the deer carcass—rubbed and torn, half-skinned, ragged but still there—up on one of the rafters in the old garage near the apartment until it hung with its back feet just touching the floor. Then I went down into the basement, where I slept on an old oversized armchair arrangement. Listening to the hiss of the coal burning in the furnace, I fell into a sleep as sound as a dead man's.

And my life moved on and there were other hunts, some better, some worse, and other deer and small game, and I did not really think of this buck again until it was time to write *Hatchet* and *Brian's Winter*, when the buck became part of Brian's life as well as mine.

CHAPTER 5

EATING EYEBALLS AND GUTS OR STARVING: THE FINE ART OF WILDERNESS NUTRITION

He looked out across the lake and brought the egg to his mouth and closed his eyes and sucked and squeezed the egg at the same time and swallowed as fast as he could. . . . It had a greasy, almost oily taste, but it was still an egg. HATCHET

There are two main drives in nature: to survive and to reproduce. But the primary drive is to survive, for reproduction cannot occur without survival. In most of nature, the most important element in survival is finding food.

I spent a lot of time in winter camps with dogs while I was training for and running the

Iditarod, and I could have learned a whole life's lesson by studying just one animal—not the dog, not the wolf, but one type of bird: the chickadee.

Chickadees are simply amazing. They do not migrate but stay north for the winter; at forty, fifty, even sixty below, they not only survive but seem to be happy, fluffed up to stay insulated and warm, and tough beyond belief. I would find frozen grouse; frozen deer standing dead, leaning against trees; frozen rabbits; and two times, even frozen men—all killed by nature, by cold, by starvation or by blatant stupidity.

(Imagine going cross-country skiing in the dead of winter in thick, old-growth forest and not even bringing a book of matches or a butane lighter; the poor fool broke his leg on a small hill and froze to death in the middle of enough fuel to heat a small city.)

But I never found a dead chickadee. They

are like little feathered wolves, except more versatile.

I'm not sure exactly when, but at some point in my youth, in the wild, I decided that if it didn't grow or live in the woods I didn't want it. For a considerable time, in a very real way, I lived not unlike Brian in *Hatchet*. I would head into the woods with nothing but my bow and a dozen arrows—eight blunts and three or four broadheads—a small package of salt, some matches and little else.

When I first started to do this I found that luck had a large part to play in whether I ate, as it did with Brian. But as with Brian, two fundamentals had a great influence on my life. The first was the concept of learning. I went from simply walking through the woods, bulling my way until something moved for me to try a shot at, to trying to understand what I saw, and from that, to "feeling" what the woods were about: a sound

here, a movement there, a line that looked out of place or curved the wrong way, a limb that moved against the wind at the wrong time or a smell that was wrong. And not just one of these things, not a single one but all of them mixed together, entered into my mind to make me a part of the woods, so that I came to know some things that were going to happen before they happened: which way a grouse would probably fly, how a rabbit or deer would run or what cover it would make for next.

This didn't come all at once—at first it was slow—but before long I understood things that I didn't quite know how I comprehended: a line would catch my eye and I would know, *know* that it was a grouse and that it was going to fly slightly up and to the left—and it would happen in just that way. I would hear a sound, just the tiniest scrape or crack of a twig, and I would *know* it was a deer and that it had seen me and would run before I could turn and get an arrow off. To learn these things, to know how all of it worked and to be part of it, was one of the great achievements in my life and has stayed with me. It has been the one guiding part of living that has helped me more than anything else. To learn, to be willing to learn how a thing works, to understand an animal in nature, or how to write a book or run a dog team or sail a boat, to always keep learning is truly wonderful.

The other truth—one that Brian came to know, and something that people all over the world have known and spoken of for thousands of years—is that hunger makes the best sauce.

Something that you would normally never consider eating, something completely repulsive and ugly and disgusting, something so gross it would make you vomit just looking at it, becomes absolutely delicious if you're starving.

Consider the British navy in the old days of sailing ships. Their principal food was hardtack, a dried biscuit kept in wooden barrels that were never quite airtight. After months and sometimes years at sea the biscuits would become full of maggots. The men had once spent many days trying to get rid of the worms, but now they were close to starving, and they saw the maggots as food to smear on the biscuits, a kind of tasty butter. They would also eat the rats that hid in the ship's hold. By the end of a long voyage the rats could be sold to hungry sailors for up to a month's wages.

When I first started living on game, I thought only of grouse and rabbits and deer. I had thought I would eat only the best parts of the animal and stay away from anything disgusting. Like guts.

And I hung in with that thinking until I went about three days without making a kill, and when I finally did, it was a red squirrel, which is about the size and edibility of the common rat, if perhaps cuter. It was sitting on a limb about twenty feet away and I caught it with a blunt and dropped it and took it back to my camp and cleaned, skinned and gutted it. And then looked at it.

It looked as if I'd skinned a gerbil. I had a small aluminum pot and I put water in it and then the small carcass and boiled it for a time with some husked acorns I found. I ate it, along with the acorns, and I was cleaning the pot when I noticed the entrails on a log where I'd left them when I gutted the squirrel. My stomach was still empty, so I took the small heart and kidneys and lungs, leaving the stomach and intestines, and I boiled up another stew and ate it with more acorns. I was still hungry. Famished. There was no way a person could get fat living on such a diet. But you wouldn't starve, either, and some of the edge of my hunger was gone.

After that I looked at food, or game, very differently. With the onset of hunger in the woods—a hunger that did not leave me unless I killed something large, such as a deer, or killed and ate more than one rabbit or three or more grouse, or as many as ten or fifteen small fish—I never again thought simply in terms of steaks or choice portions of meat or vegetation.

As the hunger increases the diet widens. I have eaten grub worms wrapped in fresh dandelion greens. They were too squishy for me to want to chew them so I swallowed them whole, but I did eat them and they stayed down. I have sucked the eyes out of fish that I caught the way Brian caught the panfish, with a homemade bow and willow arrows, sharpening the dry willow stalks and carving a shallow barb on the ends before fire-hardening them. I have also scaled fish with a spoon and then eaten the skin along with the cooked liver and brains. I ate rabbit brains, too. I have eaten snake in survival courses, and it's surprisingly good. After reading a *National Geographic* about African natives when I was a boy, I tried eating both ants and grasshoppers. I found, as with the grub worms, they are easier to eat whole, wrapped in a leaf, although cooked grasshoppers are crunchy and, if you remember the salt, aren't bad—kind of like snack food.

Once the door was opened to eating strange food, or perhaps a better phrase might be odd aspects of familiar game and fish, I found I was ready for almost anything and that almost nothing would go to waste. This is not so astonishing really, when you consider that this practice was common among natives in most early cultures, and while much of it has been forgotten because of neglect and a bounty of cheap, readily available food, there are still sources for the knowledge.

I was running my first Iditarod and pulled into a village along the Bering Sea early in the day. This in itself was strange because for some reason I seemed to arrive at all the villages in the middle of the night. But it was early, before noon, and I'd run all night and was tired, as I thought the dogs were, but they suddenly took off at a dead run, passing the checkpoint where I was to sign in, barreling down the village street until they came to a small dwelling where a little boy was kneeling over the carcass of a freshly killed seal. The dogs had smelled it, and it was only with the greatest difficulty that I finally got the snow hook buried in the packed snow and stopped them before they piled on top of the boy. I was terrified they might do him some injury—he was about six years old and small—but he seemed unconcerned and turned slowly when I pulled up. His mouth and chin were bloody and I could see that he had been sucking fresh blood out of a hole cut in the seal's neck. He smiled at me and gestured and said, "You want some?"

It was a generous offer and I didn't feel right rejecting it so I nodded and leaned down and tasted it. It was not unpleasant, although I would have preferred it cooked—as I'd eaten blood sausage, which I made by baking blood and flour in a bread pan—and I nodded and thanked him. Later I would see him walking down a passage between buildings eating straight Crisco out of a can with two fingers as if it were ice cream. Still friendly and courteous, he offered me a two-finger scoop of the white fat, but I thanked him and turned it down.

When I set out to write the Brian books I

was concerned that everything that happened to Brian should be based on reality, or as near reality as fiction could be. I did not want him to do things that wouldn't or couldn't really happen in his situation. Consequently I decided to write only of things that had happened to me or things I purposely did to make certain they would work for Brian.

One of the hardest was to start a fire with a hatchet and a rock. I cast around for days near a lake in the north woods, searching for a rock that would give off sparks when struck with the dull edge of a hatchet. I spent better than four hours getting it to work. It seemed impossible. The sparks would fly and die before they hit tinder, or they would head off in the wrong direction, or not be hot enough, or some dampness in the tinder would keep it from taking. But at last, at long last, a spark hit just right and there was a tendril of smoke and then a glowing coal and, with gentle blowing, a tiny flame, and then a fire. I can't think of many things, including Iditarods or sailing the Pacific, that affected me as deeply as getting that fire going; I felt as early man must have felt when he discovered fire, and it was very strange but I didn't want to put it out. Even though I had plenty of matches and could easily start a new fire, there was something unique, something intense and important about this one campfire.

My one failure was eating a raw turtle egg. I finished *Hatchet* in the spring, while I was running dogs and training for my first Iditarod. This was in northern Minnesota, not far from the Canadian border, in thick forest near hundreds of small lakes. It is one of the most beautiful places on earth and because of my heart trouble I can no longer take the winters up there, but I still miss it and remember my time there only with joy and wonder.

In the spring and early summer, after the snow is gone, you cannot run dogs on sleds, but there are old logging roads everywhere and you can have the dogs pull a light three-wheeled training cart. The dogs are very strong after a whole winter of training and racing and they view this as a kind of lark in which the object is to run as fast as possible down the old logging trails and to "crack the whip" on corners and flip the cart into the ditch or the brush at the side of the road. I swear they laugh when they do this. And the driver's job is to keep the cart upright while running through the forest on the narrow old trails.

That spring I ran on some new trails that I hadn't used before; the snow had gone early and the ice was out. The topsoil up there is unbelievably thin. Though there is thick forest it is like the rain forests in South America; there is heavy growth because there is so much water, not because there is rich soil. On the logging roads the soil is gone and what remains is sand, as pure as any beach sand in the world. After all, in prehistoric times, the area was one large inland sea.

The sandy roads wind through countless lakes and still ponds in the woods and in each pond there are snapping turtles. Because I had not run these roads in the spring I didn't know that the female turtles come out to lay their eggs in the sand, and the best open sand they can find is on the logging roads.

These are big turtles, some of them two or more feet across. And they are ugly, and they are very, very mean. They always make me think of what you would get if you crossed a *T. rex* with an alligator. They hiss and snap and bite and can easily take a finger off. I once had a friend named Walter who got his rear end too close to a snapper on a riverbank and I will always remember the sight of him running past me, naked, screaming, "Get it off! Get it off!" The snapper had locked, and I do mean *locked*, onto the right cheek and would not let go even when we finally stopped Walter and used a stick to try and pry the turtles jaws apart. I suspect he still has a good scar there.

One day I came barreling over a small hill around a corner thick with brush and the dogs ran directly over a female weighing about forty pounds in the process of laying eggs. Apparently she was not having a good day and we did nothing to improve her disposition. The dogs had never seen a turtle before and heaven only knows what they thought—probably that she was an alien sent down specifically to kill and eat dogs. Everything happened very fast. I saw her just as the dogs ran over her, and she snapped at them left and right, hissing and spitting fur when she connected, and then the cart flipped on its side and the dogs left the trail and tried to climb the trees alongside the road and I rolled over the top of the snapper, screaming some words I thought I had forgotten as she took a silver-dollar-sized chunk out of my jacket, and the cart gouged a hole beneath her and dug up her eggs and we all tumbled to a stop.

I lay on my stomach, four feet beyond the turtle. The dogs were scattered through the trees, still in harness and tangled so badly that I would have to use a knife to free some of them. For half a beat nothing moved or made a sound.

Then the turtle looked at the wreckage of her nest, the small round eggs scattered like dirty ping-pong balls; at me flopped there; at the dogs among the trees and the cart lying on its side, and she gave it all up as a bad try and with a final loud hiss, she dragged herself off the sandy trail and back to the swamp where she lived, looking very prehistoric and completely fed up.

As I began gathering up the pieces, my lead dog, Cookie—who was so smart and quick she never got tangled—reached around and deftly used her teeth to sever the tug holding her to the team (a habit I wished she would stop) and moved down to the turtle nest. She smelled one of the eggs, nuzzled it with her nose, then ate it whole. I knew skunks dug the nests up and ate them, because I had seen the torn-apart nests around lakes and swamps. Since I was writing *Hatchet*, it came to me that Brian would almost certainly run into a turtle nest, having crashed into a northern lake, and would be hungry enough to eat the eggs. I grabbed half a dozen of them before Cookie could eat them all. She let me have them without protesting, other than lifting her lip a bit—which should have been a warning to me that perhaps they were not as good as eggs might be—and I put them in the pocket of my jacket until I had a quiet moment.

Here we might look at several mistakes I made. First, I set myself too far away from the subject of my research: I had a full stomach; Brian was starving. Brian had just crashed in a plane; I had merely flipped over in a dog-training cart. And in the end Brian was desperate; I was only doing research.

With the dogs settled back into patched harnesses, I took out one of the eggs, cleaned the dirt off it, used my knife to cut the leathery shell slightly, and without waiting to think I tipped my head back and sucked out the contents.

I have eaten some strange things in my life: raw meat, eyeballs, guts. In the Philippines I tried to eat a local delicacy called a *baloot*, a duck egg with the baby duckling dead and fermented and half-rotten on the inside, and it all slithers out into your mouth with only a slimy lump here and there. I have eaten bugs, and I *know* that some of the food in army C rations was fermented road kill canned in lard and cigarette ashes mixed with cat vomit.

But I couldn't hold the turtle eggs down.

They hung halfway down my throat and tasted the way I imagine Vaseline would taste if, somehow, it were rotten. I looked at the horizon and thought of wonderful things, of ice cream and steak and the apple pies my grandmother used to bake for me with light-brown crusts and sugar sprinkled on top, of lobster and cheeseburgers and vanilla malts, and I lost it.

I threw up turtle eggs at terminal velocity, straight out like a runny yellow bullet, and Cookie, as if patiently waiting, licked it up, which made me throw up harder. She neatly caught the vomit before it could even hit the ground.

So it was the one bit of research I couldn't finish, though I tried three times. The second and third tries were worse, much worse, resulting in dry heaves and a snort from Cookie when nothing came. But I left it in because Brian was a different person, in a much different situation. Pushed to the limits of hunger he would probably have been able to keep the eggs down.

Even if they were slimy and yellow and tasted totally funky.

CHAPTER 6

THE JOY OF COOKING

He would not forget his first hit. Not ever. . . . He grabbed the arrow and raised it up and the fish was on the end, wiggling against the blue sky.

He held the fish against the sky until it stopped wiggling, held it and looked to the sky and felt his throat tighten, swell, and fill with pride at what he had done.

He had done food. HATCHET

We take so much for granted when it comes to eating that we almost always forget how easy we have it. When we're hungry we simply throw a package in the microwave, punch a button and eat a hot meal. Most people seem to consider "roughing it" to mean that they actually have to cook a meal—peel the potatoes, fry the steak, cut up the string beans. We forget that for most of man's history there was no such thing as a frying pan or a cooking pot or a salt shaker or a fork.

Brian lived as they did in prehistoric times, and as I have done on occasion. But even with primitive cooking methods it's possible to have relatively good food. As an example, here are a few recipes that have worked well for me.

☞ HOT WATER

Tricky without a pot, but if there is time (and there is always time if you're lost in the wilderness) you can make a pot by stitching green birch bark into a cone and using thick pine pitch (taken from lumps of pitch found on the sides of pine trees) to seal the seam of the cone. (It helps if you warm the pitch next to the fire to make it sticky, then use a twig to apply it, because once it sticks to your fingers it will be there until the skin rubs off.) This is the same technique used by Native Americans to make birch-bark canoes. One problem with a birch-bark cooking pot is that the pot doesn't last long and the pine pitch needs to be repaired constantly.

To heat water, make a forked-branch handle to hold the cone wedged in the middle, then add cold water. Heat bits of granite stone as hot as possible in a fire and, using sticks as tools, drop them in the water. Any ash will float to the surface and can be skimmed off. The water can be sipped hot (great on a cold morning) or meat can be put in to make a soup or stew.

A note about water: Of course good water is necessary for survival and bad water can kill you. The Lewis and Clark expedition headed into probably the cleanest, least-polluted wilderness in the world when they made their voyage of discovery, and yet dysentery from drinking bad water was still devastating to them. When they were boating on muddy, dirty water, they would simply dip their tin cups in the river and drink the water. They had no knowledge of bacteria or what caused disease, but they suspected dirty water. However, rather than boil it for twenty minutes before drinking it, which will kill most bacteria, the men dipped their cups well beneath the scum on the surface to get at the "pure" water down below. They had medicine with them and the one they used most was a "purgative pill" that would clean out the system "like a bomb"—which must have been incredible if given to a man who already was suffering from dysentery. The wonder is that any of them lived through it.

☞ Fish or Meat Stew

Using the same birch-bark container or one like it, put a fish or small animal in the water and keep adding and removing hot— really hot, red-hot if possible—bits of granite until the water boils, then keep adding reheated stones until the meat is cooked and falling off the bones. If it is a fish, don't skin or scale it; if it is small game, remove the hair; if it's a bird, remove the feathers but leave the innards inside. This is for two reasons. First, it actually makes the meat taste better. Second, there is much food value in liver and kidney and heart. But you might want to remove the stomach and intestines. If you do, don't waste them; strip out the digested or partially digested food, wash them in cold water, then cook both the stomach and intestines in the soup-stew you're making in the birch-bark pot. In the old days native people would pull the intestines out of an animal they had just killed and eat them raw, contents and all, sometimes sprinkling a little gall from the gallbladder on it for seasoning—this was especially true when they killed and ate buffalo.

If it's a small animal or fish, once it is cooked, drink the broth and then pick the meat off the bones and eat everything—*everything;* suck the eyes out, dig out the brain. Get over your squeamishness because it is the exact opposite of what you need to survive in the wilderness.

☞ Plank Food

Not as good as making a pot out of birch bark, but if there is no birch bark available and you don't want to eat the meat raw, this is a slightly better way of cooking than putting the meat on a stick and turning it over the fire, because spit cooking lets too much of the food drip into the fire and burn up. With plank cooking you leave the animal whole, taking off the hair or feathers. Fashion a flat piece of wood and use wooden pegs to hold the meat to the wood, then prop the plank on rocks so that it faces the heat. Let it lean there until the meat is done enough to eat. It does work, if slowly, but you don't have a broth to drink and some of the food value is lost, dripping away or soaking into the wood.

Either way, with the boiling method or plank cooking, when you are done you can use the bones for making another stew, or at least a flavored broth, if a container of some kind is available. Bird bones are hollow because birds need to be light to fly, but small-game bones have marrow and if broken and reboiled will provide more nutrition.

When dried, small bones can be useful as tools; arrowheads for small-game arrows can be fashioned from fire-hardened bones that have been filed sharp on abrasive stones. You can also use them for fishhooks when using a piece of line with bait—perhaps a grub worm that you haven't eaten yourself.

Nothing goes to waste.

☞ Spit Cooking

Maybe the first cooking ever done was done by mistake when a piece of meat or some form of plant food fell into the fire and was snaked out with a stick. It's hard to call this cooking—it's more of an accident—but it must have led to cooking on a spit.

It is not a particularly good way to cook meat—although it has evolved into shish kebab cooking, which works well at a barbecue—but it *does* get food cooked, and if done carefully and with a great deal of attention it's not so bad. The main thing to remember is to keep the meat just close enough to the fire to cook it but not so close as to burn it, and to rotate it constantly, to keep the juices from all dripping into the fire. The worst, and I mean the very *worst* piece of meat I ever had, was when I tried spit cooking a jackrabbit and didn't rotate it constantly. Jackrabbit is notoriously tough anyway, and just about the only way to cook it is to boil it until it is little more than mush, but I was in a desert and had neither cooking utensils nor birch bark to make a pot. The rabbit practically walked into my arrow and I hadn't eaten anything but two lizards for a day and a half. I finally cut the spit-roasted meat in chunks and swallowed them whole because they simply weren't chewable. I think if I had tried to chew it up before swallowing it I'd be chewing it yet. It was nutritious and kept me going but was just like chewing wood. Cottontail rabbits were plentiful and after I learned how to hunt them I never ate roasted jackrabbit again. The problem with cottontails is that they are largely nocturnal; they live in burrows during the day and are hard to hunt in daylight. The solution was shown to me by an Apache who found an old piece of barbed wire and made it into a six-foot-long crank. He would crank the wire into a rabbit hole until it tangled with the rabbit's fur, then pull out the rabbit and knock it in the head. I did this four or five times over three days. Then one morning I worked the crank into a rabbit hole, felt it hit something and pulled out about three and a half feet of really angry diamondback rattlesnake. It struck four times, somehow without touching me, while I cranked it back into the hole.

☞ Pit Cooking

Cooking in a heated pit is a very popular way to cook meat.

Dig a pit larger than the item you are going to cook and fill it with rocks, then build a roaring fire on the rocks until they are nearly red-hot. Then take the fur or feathers off the animal and wrap the meat in many layers of long grass and soft leaves (or dampened burlap, if it's available), put it on the rocks and cover the whole thing with at least a foot of dirt. Then leave it all night, or if you started in the morning, wait until late afternoon or evening, and you will find the meat tender and delicious.

I have pit-cooked grouse and rabbit and beef and mutton and pork and venison and lobster and fish (catfish, walleye, northern pike and sea bass, and tuna wrapped in seaweed) and loved them all, and in the end I think this is probably my favorite way of wilderness cooking—with one exception.

I was helping as a laborer on a really bad movie about mountain men, so bad that it was never released. This was years before the present regulations governing animal use existed. Part of the film involved shooting and killing a buffalo, which had been purchased from a nearby ranch. This was done poorly, and the meat would have gone to waste because nobody in the crew seemed to know what to do after the buffalo was killed. I found a butcher knife in one of the catering wagons and before they could drag the carcass off I cut a line down the back, peeled the skin back (it was incredibly thick and tough) and cut out about a ten-pound hump roast and five or six pounds of tenderloin from next to the backbone.

One of the associate producers saw me cutting away and confiscated the tenderloin but he left me the hump, so I made a fire near the movie location, which was out in the desert. I was camped in an old army tent and I cooked the whole hump over a bed of mesquite coals, turning it constantly, and I have never tasted meat that good. The smoky taste, mixed with rich fat and a touch of wildness, made it incredibly good. I had a friend working on the film and the two of us sat there and ate the whole thing, cutting off slabs of meat with the borrowed butcher knife, and washed it down with glasses of pure spring water.

It was a grand feast, a feast that made me think of ancient people and how they must have been before there was writing, before there was recorded history, when they sat this way by old fires, cutting meat with stone tools, looking up at the stars and letting the food and fire fill them with life. It was probably the closest I have ever come to being a cave painting, except when I ran my first

Iditarod and let the dogs carry me back in time. In a strange way, although my buffalo feast was in barren desert and not northern woods and lakes, it might have been the time when I was closest to Brian in *Hatchet* and *Brian's Winter*. It would be eight more years until I would move north and run dogs and trap wild animals and begin the process of actually writing about Brian, but it all started when I ate the buffalo hump by the fire.

What if, I asked myself that night, looking into the flames. What if a person suddenly found himself in a wilderness as old as time . . .